Published simultaneously in 1998 by Exley Publications Ltd. in
Great Britain, and Exley Publications LLC in the USA.

12 11 10 9 8 7 6 5 4 3 2 1

**Edited and pictures selected by Helen Exley**
**ISBN 1-86187-061-2**

Printed in Hungary.

**Exley Publications Ltd, 16 Chalk Hill, Watford,**
**Herts WD1 4BN, UK.**
**Exley Publications LLC, 232 Madison Avenue,**
**Suite 1206, NY 10016, USA.**

# Words on Strength and Perseverance

A HELEN EXLEY
GIFTBOOK

**EXLEY**

NEW YORK • WATFORD, UK

**Y**ou can have
anything you want
if you want it
desperately enough.
You must want it
with an exuberance
that erupts through
the skin and joins
the energy that
created the world.

SHELIA GRAHAM

**W**hen you have gone so far

that you can't manage

one more step, then you've

gone just half the distance

that you're capable of.

GREENLAND
PROVERB

There are really only two ways
to approach life: as victim
or as gallant fighter.
You must decide if you want
to act or react.
Deal your own cards or play
with a stacked deck.
And if you don't decide
which way to play with life,
it always plays with you.

MERLE SHAIN

# YOU ARE THE ARCHITECT
## OF YOUR PERSONAL
### EXPERIENCE.

SHIRLEY MACLAINE,
b.1934

DO WHAT YOU
CAN, WITH WHAT
YOU HAVE,
WHERE YOU ARE.

THEODORE ROOSEVELT
(1858-1919)

*T*here is no such thing
as a great talent
without great will-power.

HONORE DE BALZAC

(1799-1850)

Life is not easy for any of us.
But what of that? We must have
perseverance and above all
confidence in ourselves.

*We must believe that we are gifted for something, and that this thing, at whatever cost, must be attained.*

MARIE CURIE (1867-1934)

*... if you want something very badly, you can achieve it. It may take patience, very hard work, a real struggle, and a long time; but it can be done. That much faith is a prerequisite of any undertaking, artistic or otherwise.*

MARGO JONES (1913-1955)

*I LONG TO ACCOMPLISH*

*A GREAT AND NOBLE TASK,*

*BUT IT IS MY CHIEF DUTY*

*TO ACCOMPLISH SMALL TASKS*

*AS IF THEY WERE GREAT*

*AND NOBLE.*

HELEN KELLER
(1880-1968)

I don't think of myself
as a poor deprived
ghetto girl who made good.
I think of myself as
somebody who from an
early age knew
I was responsible for myself,
and I had to make good.

OPRAH WINFREY

*T*he world has no room for
cowards. We must all be
ready somehow to toil, to
suffer, to die. And yours is
not the less noble because no
drum beats before you when

*you go out into your daily battlefields, and no crowds shout about your coming when you return from your daily victory or defeat.*

ROBERT LOUIS STEVENSON (1850-1894)

I don't say embrace trouble.
That's as bad as treating it
as an enemy. But I do say
meet it as a friend,
for you'll see a lot of it
and had better be on
speaking terms with it.

OLIVER WENDELL HOLMES, JR

ALTHOUGH THE WORLD
IS VERY FULL OF SUFFERING,
IT IS ALSO FULL
OF THE OVERCOMING OF IT.

HELEN KELLER

(1880-1968)

*Know how sublime
a thing it is to suffer
and be strong.*

HENRY

WADSWORTH

LONGFELLOW

(1807-1882)

*A* saint is not one
who never falls; it is one
who gets up and goes on
every time he falls.

AUTHOR UNKNOWN

*TO BECOME
A CHAMPION, FIGHT
ONE MORE ROUND*

JAMES J. CORBETT

*You never really lose
until you quit trying.*

MIKE DITKA

*Whether you think
you can or you can't,
you're right!*

HENRY FORD (1863-1947)

# nOTHING
## IS SO STRONG
## AS GENTLENESS;
## NOTHING
## SO GENTLE
## AS REAL
## STRENGTH.

*ST FRANCIS DE SALES*

*(1567-1622)*

You gotta play the hand that's dealt you. There may be pain in that hand, but you play it.

JAMES BRADY

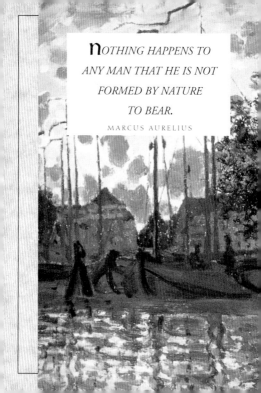

NOTHING HAPPENS TO
ANY MAN THAT HE IS NOT
FORMED BY NATURE
TO BEAR.

MARCUS AURELIUS

**S**uccess seems to be largely
a matter of hanging on after
others have let go.

WILLIAM FEATHER

Stand through life firm
as a rock in the sea,
undisturbed and unmoved
by its ever-rising waves.

HAZRAT INAYAT KHAN

no matter how bad
things got, my mother
made it clear
that we were not defined
by our financial situation.
We were defined by
our ability to overcome it.

ANNA PEREZ

The power to hold on in spite of everything, the power to endure — this is the winner's quality. Persistence is the ability to face defeat again and again without giving up — to push on in the face of great difficulty, knowing that victory can be yours. Persistence means taking pains to overcome every obstacle, and to do what's necessary to reach your goals.

WYNN DAVIS,
FROM "THE BEST OF SUCCESS"

Life only demands
from the strength
you possess.
Only one feat
is possible – not to
have to run away.

DAG HAMMARSKJOLD

Without belittling the courage with which men have died, we should not forget those acts of courage with which men... have lived. The courage of life is often a less dramatic spectacle than the courage of a final moment; but it is no less a magnificent mixture of triumph and tragedy. A man does what he must — in spite of personal consequences, in spite of obstacles and dangers and pressures — and that is the basis of all human morality....

*JOHN F. KENNEDY*

*Every step toward the goal of justice requires sacrifice, suffering, and struggle; the tireless exertion and passionate concerns of dedicated individuals.*

MARTIN LUTHER KING

*Hate cannot destroy hate,*
*but love can and does.*
*Not the soft and negative*
*thing that has carried the*
*name and misrepresented*
*the emotion, but love that*
*suffers all things and is*
*kind, love that accepts*
*responsibility, love that*
*marches, love that suffers,*
*love that bleeds and dies*
*for a great cause — but to*
*rise again.*

DANIEL A. POLING

*For* people sometimes believed
that it was safer
to live with complaints,
was necessary to cooperate
with grief, was all right
to become an accomplice in
self-ambush.... Take heart to
flat out decide to be well
and stride into the future
sane and whole.

TONI CADE BAMBARA

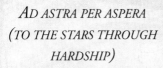

*AD ASTRA PER ASPERA*
*(TO THE STARS THROUGH*
*HARDSHIP)*

MOTTO OF
THE STATE OF KANSAS

Behold, we live through all things, – famine, thirst, bereavement, pain; all grief and misery, all woe and sorrow; life inflicts its worst on soul and body, – but we cannot die, though we be sick, and tired, and tired, and faint, and worn, lo, all things can be borne!

ELIZABETH AKERS ALLEN

*A*nd so what I've learned in the last twenty years is that *I* am the sole judge and jury about what my limits will be. And as I look toward the horizon of the next twenty years, it is *no... no* limit. With that kind of knowledge, I've grown as old as I can possibly be; the ageing has stopped here, and now I just grow better.

GLORIA NAYLOR

**Y**ou shall be free
indeed when your days
are not without a care
nor your nights without
a want and a grief.
But rather when these
things girdle your life
and yet you rise above
them naked and
unbound.

KAHLIL GIBRAN
(1883-1931)

We perceive that only through utter defeat are we able to take our first steps towards liberation and strength. Our admissions of personal powerlessness finally turn out to be a firm bedrock upon which happy and purposeful lives may be built.

BILL WILSON

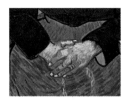

*I WILL BE
CONQUERED;
I WILL NOT
CAPITULATE.*

SAMUEL JOHNSON
(1709-1784),
ON HIS ILLNESS

The thought that we are enduring the unendurable is one of the things that keep us going.

MOLLY HASKELL

**P**erseverance is not
a long race; it is many short
races one after another.

WALTER ELLIOTT,
FROM "THE SPIRITUAL LIFE"

*I am a kind of burr;
I shall stick.*

WILLIAM SHAKESPEARE

(1564-1616)

*In the depth
of winter,
I finally learned
that within me
there lay
an invincible
summer.*

ALBERT CAMUS
(1913-1960)

*Whatever life's challenges you may face, remember always to look to the mountaintop, for in so doing you look to greatness. Remember this, and let no problem, no matter how great it may seem, discourage you, nor let anything less than the mountaintop distract you. This is the one thought I want to leave you with.*

ALFONSO ORTIZ

**m**y will shall shape my future. Whether I fail or succeed shall be no man's doing but my own. I am the force; I can clear any obstacle

*before me or I can be lost
in the maze. My choice;
my responsibility; win or lose,
only I hold the key to
my destiny.*

ELAINE MAXWELL

**Acknowledgements:** The publishers are grateful for permission to reproduce copyright material. Whilst every reasonable effort has been made to trace copyright holders, the publishers would be pleased to hear from any not here acknowledged. KAHLIL GIBRAN: from *The Prophet* © 1923 Kahlil Gibran, renewed © 1951 Administrators C.T.A of Kahlil Gibran Estate and Mary Gibran. Published by Knopf, New York 1961. GLORIA NAYLOR: from *Interview / Talks with America's Writing Women* by Mickey Pearlman and Katherine Henderson. Published by The University Press of Kentucky © 1990. ALFONSO ORTIZ: from Look To The Mountaintop in *Essays on Reflection,* edited by E. Graham, published by Houghton-Mifflin 1973.

**Picture credits:** Exley Publications would like to thank the following organizations and individuals for permission to reproduce their pictures. Whilst every reasonable effort has been made to trace copyright holders, the publishers would be pleased to hear from any not here acknowledged. Archiv für Kunst (AKG), Artworks, Bridgeman Art Library (BAL), Edimedia (EDM), Fine Art Photographic Library (FAP), Giraudon, Peter Kettle, Scala, Statens Konstmuseer, Stockholm, SuperStock (SS).

Cover and Title Page: Vincent Van Gogh, *Enclosed Field With Rising Sun,* SS; pages 6/7: Artist unknown; pages 8/9: © 1998 Peter Kettle, page 11: *Portrait of Fernando Amorsolo;* pages 12/13: Ilyich Chistyakov, *Young Woman,* BAL; page 15: L. Hermitte, *Portrait of Edouard Manet,* Giraudon; pages 16/17: Ivan Constantowitsch Aivazoffski, *The*